THE OFFICIAL
OUTLANDER
COLORING BOOK

VOLUME 2

AN ADULT COLORING BOOK

DIANA GABALDON

BANTAM
NEW YORK

A Bantam Books Trade Paperback Original

Copyright © 2023 by Diana Gabaldon
Text copyright © 1992 by Diana Gabaldon

Published in the United States by Bantam Books, an imprint of
Random House, a division of Penguin Random House LLC, New York.

BANTAM BOOKS & B colophon is a registered trademark of Penguin Random House LLC.

Illustration credits
Mélanie Delon: pages 11, 25, 31, 49, 57, 81
Ana Jarén: pages 7, 19, 21, 65, 69, 79, 83, 85, 87
Matthew Land: pages 5, 37, 39, 43, 55, 93
Ben Perini: pages 15, 23, 53, 59, 61, 71, 75, 89
Monika Roe: pages 9, 13, 17, 29, 33, 41, 47, 51, 63, 67, 73, 77, 91
Cat Willett: pages 27, 35, 45

ISBN 978-0-593-59461-2

The text in this work originally appeared in *Dragonfly in Amber* by Diana Gabaldon,
published by Bantam Books, an imprint of Random House, a division of
Penguin Random House LLC in 1992.

Printed in the United States of America on acid-free paper

randomhousebooks.com

1st Printing

Title page art by Liudmyla © Adobe Stock Photos

Book design by Sara Bereta

THE OFFICIAL
OUTLANDER
COLORING BOOK

VOLUME 2

We set off at once in Jared's wake, sidestepping the rumbling traffic of casks and hogsheads, carts and barrows, and men and boys of all descriptions carrying bolts of fabric, boxes of grain and foodstuffs, rolls of hammered copper, sacks of flour, and anything else that could be transported by ship. Le Havre was an important center of shipping traffic, and the docks were the heart of the city.

A prosperous Scottish émigré, Jared was an importer of wines and spirits, with a small warehouse and large town house in Paris, and a very large warehouse indeed here in Le Havre, where he had asked Jamie to meet him, when Jamie had written to say we were en route to Paris.

"And you were in France," Roger murmured as though to himself, still studying me closely. The shock in his face was fading into surmise, and a kind of excitement. "I don't suppose you knew . . ."

"Yes, I did," I told him. "That's why we went to Paris. I'd told Jamie about Culloden—the '45, and what would happen. We went to Paris to try to stop Charles Stuart."

It was a large group of people, men and women, soberly clad by comparison with the bright colors of the courtiers around them. It was the sound of them, though, rather than the appearance, that had caught my attention. French, spoken by a number of people at a distance, strongly resembles the quacking conversation of ducks and geese, with its nasal elements. English, on the other hand, has a slower pace, and much less rise and fall in its intonations. Spoken at a distance where individual voices are impossible to distinguish, it has the gruff, friendly monotony of a sheepdog's barking. And the general effect of the mass exodus presently coming in our direction was of a gaggle of geese being driven to market by a pack of dogs.

"Aye, it's France," he agreed. "Food, and drink—and love."

To my annoyance, I lacked several of the herbs I needed for the sleeping tonic I had in mind. But then I remembered the man Marguerite had told me about. Raymond the herb-seller, in the Rue de Varenne. A wizard, she had said. A place worth seeing.

Jamie, immersed in a handful of shipping orders, glanced up at the sound and froze, eyes wide. His mouth opened, but he made no sound.

"How do you like it?" Handling the train a bit gingerly, I stepped down into the room, swaying gently as the seamstress had instructed, to show off the filmy gussets of silk plissé let into the overskirt.

Jamie shut his mouth and blinked several times.

"It's . . . ah . . . red, isn't it?" he observed.

"Rather." *Sang-du-Christ,* to be exact. Christ's blood, the most fashionable color of the season, or so I had been given to understand.

The guests wandered to and fro, conversing, admiring the paintings on the walls, flirting behind fans, consuming confits, tartlets, and wine, and disappearing at more or less discreet intervals into the odd little curtained alcoves. These were cleverly fitted into the paneling of the rooms, so that you scarcely noticed them, unless you got close enough to hear the sounds inside.

The pigeons were courting on the grass below a flowering forsythia bush. The ladies and gentlemen of the Court were performing similar activities on the paths that led through the sculpture gardens. The major difference was that the pigeons were quieter about it.

"Rook to queen's pawn five," Jamie mumbled later that evening as we prepared for bed. We were staying as guests in the palace once more. As the chess game had lasted well past midnight, and the Minister would not hear of our undertaking the journey back to Paris at such an hour, we had been accommodated in a small *appartement*—this one a notch or two above the first, I noted. It had a featherbed, and a window overlooking the south parterre.

"Rooks, eh?" I said, sliding into the bed and stretching out with a groan. "Are you going to dream about chess tonight?"

Jamie nodded, with a jaw-cracking yawn that made his eyes water.

"Aye, I'm sure I will. I hope it willna disturb ye, Sassenach, if I castle in my sleep."

How did one stop a rebellion? Well, if risings were fomented in taverns, perhaps they could be stopped over dinner tables.

He jerked his head toward the shelf that ran along the wall just above eye height. It was lined with white fired-porcelain jars, each ornamented with gilded curlicues, painted flowers and beasts, and a label, written in elaborate black script. Three of the jars closest to me were labeled in Latin, which I translated with some difficulty—crocodile's blood, and the liver and bile of the same beast, presumably the one swinging sinisterly overhead in the draft from the main shop.

"Not bad, Bouton," I said, with a nod of acknowledgment. A long pink tongue lolled happily, and the black nostrils sniffed in my direction.

"Yes, she's a good one," said Mother Hildegarde, and this time there was no doubt which of us she was speaking to, Bouton being male. Bouton leaned forward and sniffed politely at my hand, then licked my knuckles once in reciprocal acknowledgment of a fellow professional. I repressed the urge to wipe my hand on my gown.

"Amazing," I said, meaning it.

"Yes," said Mother Hildegarde, casually, but with an unmistakable note of pride. "He's very good at locating tumors beneath the skin, as well."

"Oh, yes. My godfather—the Old Sun King," she added casually, "gave to me a book of the Lives of the Saints for my own Saint's Day when I was eight. It was a beautiful book," she said reminiscently, "with gilded pages and a jeweled cover; intended more as a work of art than a work of literature. Still, I read it."

Jamie smiled suddenly at me, and stretched out a hand.

"I'll think of something, Sassenach. For now, give me your feet. Jenny said it helped to have me rub her feet when she was wi' child."

I didn't argue, but slipped my feet out of the hot shoes and swung them up onto his lap with a sigh of relief as the air from the window cooled the damp silk over my toes.

His hands were big, and his fingers at once strong and gentle. He rubbed his knuckles down the arch of my foot and I leaned back with a soft moan. We rode silently for several minutes, while I relaxed into a state of mindless bliss.

It would be a beautiful day, I could tell, the spring air ripening with warmth, and the plum blossoms bursting pink and white and bee-rich in the gardens of Versailles. The courtiers would be outside in the gardens today, rejoicing in the weather as much as the barrowmen who wheeled their wares through the streets.

So did I rejoice, alone and not alone, in my peaceful cocoon of warmth and quiet.

"Hello," I said softly, one hand over the butterfly wings that beat inside me.

Swinging around, I spotted Fergus, crouched on a stool in front of the fire, industriously stuffing pastries into his face. "Good lad," I said, smiling at him. He grinned back at me, cheeks puffed like a chipmunk's with chestnut tart.

"Are you all right, Madame?" The light hazel eyes held only respectful concern, the fine dark brows arched over them in inquiry. It wasn't Frank, of course. Neither was it Jonathan Randall. This man was younger than the Captain by a good ten years, perhaps close to my own age, his face pale and unlined by exposure to weather. His lips had the same chiseled lines, but lacked the marks of ruthlessness that bracketed the Captain's mouth.

"You. . . ." I croaked, leaning away from him. "You're . . ."

"Alexander Randall, Esquire, Madame," he answered quickly, making an abortive gesture toward his head, as though to doff a hat he wasn't wearing. "I don't believe we have met?" he said, with a hint of doubt.

It kept creeping back, though, bubbling up whenever my guard was down, as it was now. How could he do this? my mind kept muttering, in a cold fury. I shouldn't be here; I should be home, resting quietly by Jamie's side. I shouldn't have to be pursuing him, preventing him, fighting both anger and illness. A nagging pain from the coach ride knotted at the base of my spine. Yes, he might well be upset; I could understand that. But it was a man's *life* at stake, for God's sake. How could his bloody pride be more important than that? And to leave me, with no word of explanation! To leave me to find out from the gossip of neighbors what had happened.

"You promised me, Jamie, damn you, you *promised* me!" I whispered, under my breath.

I heard them before I saw them; they had started. The clash of metal was muffled by the wet shrubbery, but clear enough, nonetheless. No birds sang in the wet dawn, but the deadly voice of battle rang in my ears.

It was a large clearing, deep in the Bois, but accessible by path and road. Large enough to accommodate the footwork needed for a serious duel. They were stripped to their shirts, fighting in the rain, the wet fabric clinging, showing the outline of shoulder and backbone.

"Why do you call me madonna still?" I asked. My hands rested on the slight concavity of my stomach, gently as though not to disturb the shattering emptiness. "I've lost my child."

He looked mildly surprised.

"Ah. I did not call you madonna because you were with child, my lady."

"Why, then?" I didn't really expect him to answer, but he did. Tired and drained as we both were, it was as though we were suspended together in a place where neither time nor consequence existed; there was room for nothing but truth between us.

He sighed.

"Everyone has a color about them," he said simply. "All around them, like a cloud. Yours is blue, madonna. Like the Virgin's cloak. Like my own."

The gauze curtain fluttered briefly and he was gone.

Lallybroch absorbed Jamie at once, as though he had never left, and I found myself pulled effortlessly into the current of farm life as well. It was an unsettled autumn, with frequent rain, but with fair, bright days that made the blood sing, too. The place bustled with life, everyone hurrying through the harvest time and the preparations that must be made for the coming winter.

Willie, Jamie's elder brother, had died of the smallpox at the age of eleven, leaving his small brother, aged six, as the heir to Lallybroch.

He made an odd half-shrugging gesture, as though seeking to ease the pressure of his shirt across his shoulders. It was something he did when feeling awkward or unsure; I hadn't seen him do it in months.

"But Willie died. And so I am laird." He glanced at me, a little shyly, then reached into his sporran and pulled something out. A little cherrywood snake that Willie had carved for him as a birthday gift lay on his palm, head twisted as though surprised to see the tail following it.

Jamie stroked the little snake gently; the wood was shiny and seasoned with handling, the curves of the body gleaming like scales in early twilight.

"Jamie," she said. Her face was very pale. "There's only the one thing ye *can* do, my dearie. Ye must go and fight for Charles Stuart. Ye must help him win."

The truth of her words penetrated slowly through the layers of shock that wrapped me. The publication of this Bond of Association branded those who signed it as rebels, and as traitors to the English crown. It didn't matter now how Charles had managed, or where he had gotten the funds to begin; he was well and truly launched on the seas of rebellion, and Jamie—and I—were launched with him, willy-nilly. There was, as Jenny had said, no choice.

The weather was unseasonably warm for November, and the omnipresent clouds had broken, letting a fugitive autumn sun shine briefly on the grayness of Edinburgh. I had taken advantage of the transient warmth to be outside, however briefly, and was crawling on my knees through the rock garden behind Holyrood, much to the amusement of several Highlanders hanging about the grounds, enjoying the sunshine in their own manner, with a jug of homebrewed whisky.

"Art huntin' *burras,* Mistress?" called one man.

"Nay, it'll be fairies, surely, not caterpillars," joked another.

"You're more likely to find fairies in that jug than I am under rocks," I called back.

The man held the jug up, closed one eye, and squinted theatrically into its depths.

Closing my eyes, I felt the thrum of the music vibrating through the wooden floor, from the cellos resting on it. . . .

Jamie sat down on a vacant seat beside me, mopping his glowing face with a large white handkerchief. He reached past me to the small table, where a tray with a few leftover cakes was sitting.

"I'm fair starved," he said. "Dancing gives ye a terrible appetite."

On the far side of the long, tapestry-hung room was an enormous marble fireplace, lined with white Delft tiles, painted with Dutch country scenes in shades of blue and mulberry. . . .

Colum MacKenzie's eyes hadn't changed; neither had his voice. Both held the essence of the man who had led clan MacKenzie for thirty years, despite the disease that had crippled him in his teens. Everything else had changed sadly for the worse, though; the black hair streaked heavily with gray, the lines of his face cut deep into skin that had fallen slack over the sharp outlines of bone.

Scottish clansmen fought according to their ancient traditions. Disdaining strategy, tactics, and subtlety, their method of attack was simplicity itself. Spotting the enemy within range, they dropped their plaids, drew their swords, and charged the foe, shrieking at the tops of their lungs. Gaelic shrieking being what it is, this method was more often successful than not. A good many enemies, seeing a mass of hairy, bare-limbed banshees bearing down on them, simply lost all nerve and fled.

His Highness Prince Charles Edward bent his head under the lintel to enter the cottage. Come to visit the wounded, he was dressed for the occasion in plum velvet breeches with stockings to match, immaculate linen, and—to show solidarity with the troops, no doubt—a coat and waistcoat in Cameron tartan, with a subsidiary plaid looped over one shoulder through a cairngorm brooch. His hair was freshly powdered, and the Order of St. Andrew glittered brilliantly upon his breast.

The leaves beneath the smooth wool made a surprisingly comfortable mattress, though at this point I would cheerfully have slept on a bed of nails. I relaxed bonelessly against him, reveling in the exquisite delight of simply lying down. . . .

   The sun had reached our pile of leaves, and my shoulders relaxed under the warming touch of the light. Everything seemed slightly tinged with gold, the mingled result of early autumn and extreme fatigue. . . . All the terror and the tiredness and the noise of the two days past ebbed slowly away, leaving us alone together.

Jamie uttered a short laugh, and turned to face his grandfather. He leaned back against the table, hands braced behind him. Despite the differences in posture and figure, there was a tension between the two men that brought out a fugitive resemblance between them. The one tall and the other squat, but both of them strong, stubborn, and determined to win this encounter.

The death of Charles Stuart would not end the matter of the Rising; things had gone much too far for that. Lord George Murray, Balmerino, Kilmarnock, Lochiel, Clanranald—all of us were traitors, lives and property forfeit to the Crown. The Highland army was in tatters; without the figurehead of Charles to rally to, it would dissipate like smoke. The English, terrorized and humiliated at Preston and Falkirk, would not hesitate to pursue the fugitives, seeking to retrieve their lost honor and wash out the insult in blood.

Suddenly thinking of something, I turned to look at the harpsichord in the corner of the room. Several sheets of music adorned its rack, written in a fine, clear hand. *Fifty thousand pounds, upon the occasion of Your Highness's setting foot in Scotland.* Signed *S.* "S," of course, for Sandringham. The Duke laughed, in apparent delight.

"That was really very clever of you, my dear. It must have been you; I'd heard of your husband's unfortunate inability with music."

The pipers of the clans took it in turns to call the dawn at Stirling, walking to and fro in the encampment with the piper's measured stride, so that the wail of the drones bounced from the flimsy tents, calling all within to the battle of the new day.

Again in the evening a single piper would come out, strolling slow across the yard, and the camp would stop to listen, voices stilling and the glow of the sunset fading from the tents' canvas. The high, whining notes of the pibroch called down the shadows from the moor, and when the piper was done, the night had come.

"Claire," he said quietly. "Tomorrow I will die. This child . . . is all that will be left of me—ever. I ask ye, Claire—I beg you—see it safe."

I stood still, vision blurring, and in that moment, I heard my heart break. It was a small, clean sound, like the snapping of a flower's stem.

At last I bent my head to him, the wind grieving in my ears. . . .

"I will find you," he whispered in my ear. "I promise. If I must endure two hundred years of purgatory, two hundred years without you—then that is my punishment, which I have earned for my crimes. For I have lied, and killed, and stolen; betrayed and broken trust. But there is the one thing that shall lie in the balance. When I shall stand before God, I shall have one thing to say, to weigh against the rest."

His voice dropped, nearly to a whisper, and his arms tightened around me.

"Lord, ye gave me a rare woman, and God! I loved her well."

The clan stones were large boulders of gray granite, rounded by weather and blotched with lichens. They sat on patches of smooth grass, widely scattered near the edge of the moor. Each one bore a single name, the carving so faded by weather as to be nearly illegible in some cases. MacGillivray. MacDonald. Fraser. Grant. Chisholm. MacKenzie.

"Look," Brianna said, almost in a whisper. She pointed at one of the stones. A small heap of greenish-gray twigs lay there; a few early spring flowers mingled, wilted, with the twigs.

"Heather," Roger said. "It's more common in the summer, when the heather is blooming—then you'll see heaps like that in front of every clan stone. Purple, and here and there a branch of the white heather—the white is for luck, and for kingship; it was Charlie's emblem, that and the white rose."

For I had come back, and I dreamed once more, in the cool air of the Highlands. And the voice of my dream still echoed through ears and heart.

She carried herself like a queen, not slumping as tall girls so often do. Noting her mother's straight back and graceful posture, he could see where that particular attribute had come from. But not the remarkable height, the cascade of waist-length red hair, sparked with gold and copper, streaked with amber and cinnamon, curling casually around face and shoulders like a mantle. The eyes, so dark a blue as almost to be black in some lights. Nor that wide, generous mouth, with a full lower lip that invited nibbling kisses and biting passion. Those things must have come from her father.

Beautiful hands, Roger noted; delicately molded, carefully kept, with a single ring on each hand. The silver one on her right hand was especially striking; a wide Jacobean band in the Highland interlace pattern, embellished with thistle blossoms.

"A *rat!* You have *rats* in here?" Brianna's agitation was noticeable.

"Well, I hope not, because if so, they'll have been chewing up the records we're looking for," Roger replied. He handed her the torch. "Here, shine this in any dark places; at least you won't be taken by surprise."

"Thanks a lot." Brianna accepted the torch, but still eyed the stacks of cartons with some reluctance.

"Well, go on then," Roger said. "Or did you want me to do you a rat satire on the spot?"

Brianna's face split in a wide grin. "A rat satire? What's that?"

The door opened and Fiona Graham came in, pushing a tea cart, fully equipped with teapot, cups, doilies, three kinds of sandwiches, cream-cakes, sponge cake, jam tarts, and scones with clotted cream.

The sheer intensity of his feelings seemed to echo in the empty place. He hoped she couldn't hear them. They had known each other barely a week, after all, and had had scarcely any private conversation. She would be taken aback, surely, or frightened, if she knew what he felt. Or worse yet, she would laugh.

Yet, when he stole a glance at her, her face was calm and serious. It was also looking back at him, with an expression in the dark blue of her eyes that turned him toward her and made him reach for her without conscious thought.

The kiss was brief and gentle, scarcely more than the formality that concludes a wedding, yet as striking in its impact as though they had this minute plighted a troth.

Roger's hands fell away, but the warmth of her lingered, in hands and lips and body, so that he felt as though he held her still.

Claire's voice came from behind him, strong and urgent, shattering the silence.

"Gillian!" she called.

There was a soft, sudden whoosh, and the night lit up in brilliance. Dazzled, Roger fell back a pace, stumbling and dropping to his knees. . . .

The slim figure stood between them and the fire, silhouetted like an hourglass. As his sight cleared, he realized that she was dressed in a long, full skirt and tight bodice—the clothes of another time. She had turned at the call, and he had a brief impression of wide eyes and fair, flying hair, lifted and tossed in the hot wind of the fire.

"One man, a Fraser of the Master of Lovat's regiment, escaped. . . ." Roger repeated softly. He looked up from the stark page to see her eyes, wide and unseeing as a deer's fixed in the headlights of an oncoming car.

"He meant to die on Culloden Field," Roger whispered. "But he didn't."

Alive, and one. We are one, and while we love, death will never touch us.

ARTIFACTS FOUND ON
CULLODEN BATTLEFIELD

ABOUT THE AUTHOR

DIANA GABALDON is the #1 *New York Times* bestselling author of the wildly popular Outlander novels—*Outlander, Dragonfly in Amber, Voyager, Drums of Autumn, The Fiery Cross, A Breath of Snow and Ashes* (for which she won a Quill Award and the Corine International Book Prize), *An Echo in the Bone, Written in My Own Heart's Blood,* and *Go Tell the Bees That I Am Gone*—as well as the related Lord John Grey books, *Lord John and the Private Matter, Lord John and the Brotherhood of the Blade, Lord John and the Hand of Devils,* and *The Scottish Prisoner;* a collection of novellas, *Seven Stones to Stand or Fall;* three works of nonfiction, *"I Give You My Body . . ."* and *The Outlandish Companion Volumes 1* and *2;* and the Outlander graphic novel *The Exile.* She lives in Scottsdale, Arizona, with her husband.

dianagabaldon.com
Facebook.com/AuthorDianaGabaldon
Twitter: @Writer_DG

ABOUT THE ILLUSTRATORS

MÉLANIE DELON

alanlynchartists.com/melanie-delon

MÉLANIE DELON lives and works in a small city near Paris where she creates imagery for publishing and gaming clients around the world. Delon favors fantasy subjects with a touch of classicism and romanticism. After studying history of art and archeology at the Sorbonne, Delon transitioned to 3D digital illustration and shortly thereafter traded in her pens and paper for Photoshop and a Wacom tablet.

ANA JARÉN

anajaren.com

ANA JARÉN is a Spanish illustrator who has loved drawing since she was a child. Jarén began her career in a fashion press office, and her creativity and passion for drawing led her into illustration. She works by hand, using markers, pencils, and acrylics to beautifully capture life, people, and daily activities, always with a sharp eye for small details. Her illustrations, often of women, are inspired by popular culture and take the viewer on an evocative journey that reflects their own emotional experiences.

MATTHEW LAND

arenaillustration.com/artists/matthew-land

MATTHEW LAND grew up on a dairy farm in the Welsh hills where he read and drew almost compulsively. After graduating from University College Falmouth in 2012 and wanting a change of scene, Land moved to Edinburgh and worked as a children's bookseller in Blackwell's Bookshop. Land is influenced by heroes from the golden age of British book illustration, including Arthur Rackham, Beatrix Potter, and William Heath Robinson. He utilizes ink line work and watercolor and a touch of digital tweaking to breathe life into his unusual characters.

BEN PERINI

thinkben.com

BEN PERINI has been a professional illustrator for forty years and an artist his whole life. He is known for bringing together traditional draftsman's training and an eye for striking visuals. His work has ranged from rock band posters to videogame covers to book jackets to gallery fine art—yet this ink drawing is something new and quite a lot of fun.

MONIKA ROE

monikaroe.com

MONIKA ROE is a born creative, an award-winning illustrator, and native Californian. Her studio is located at the end of a winding road in a redwood forest overlooking Silicon Valley where she creates for clients worldwide. Known for her fashionable and imaginative approach, she continually brings ideas to life in the areas of advertising, publishing, branding, typography, greeting cards, children's products, and many more. Roe has a passion for cooking, likes browsing estate sales, and loves finding inspiration on long road trips.

CAT WILLETT

catherinewillett.com

CAT WILLETT is a Brooklyn-based artist. She is the author and illustrator of the graphic biography *The Queen of Wands: The Story of Pamela Colman Smith, the Artist Behind the Rider-Waite Tarot Deck,* published by Running Press. Willett holds her MFA from the Fashion Institute of Technology in illustration. Her illustration work runs the spectrum of books, comics, murals, editorial work, and merchandise, always with the aim of uplifting others.